SO TELL US, CHRIST

✣ ✣ ✣

Poems by Pavel Chichikov

GREY OWL PRESS

© 2015 by Pavel Chichikov

Grey Owl Press
http://pavelspoetry.com

All rights reserved. Published July 2015

Printed in the United States of America
Cover image: El Greco, "El Salvador," Museo del Greco

ISBN: 0967190169
ISBN-13: 9780967190167
Library of Congress Control Number: 2015942325
∞ Printed on acid-free paper

Contents

So Tell Us, Christ 1
The Break of Day 2
As He Loves the Jewel Starts to Blaze 4
Even in Old Babylon 5
Where It Should 6
The Curtain 7
Where Love Has Gone 8
The Dust 9
Looking Down 11
Every Power 12
When All the Wounds Cried Out 13
Brief Spring 14
If and When 15
Suddenly at Dawn and Since 16
It Is Near 18
The Space of Nothing 19
She Hates to See the Possums 20
Concealed from Whom? 21
When I Awake Again 22
Tenebrae 23
When I Showed 24
I Will Dip You in the Sky 25
I Remember 26
The Men of Sodom 27
The Mighty Doors 28
Something Marvelous 29
Or Was He Real? 30
More Bright Than Many Suns 31
The Elevation of the Host 32
The Falconry of Mammon 33
Two Rivers 34
Present Tense 35
The Groves of Glory 36

The Strangest Thing of All	37
He May Reply	38
All Admired Babylon	40
Where They Wait	41
Where Is He?	42
The Twilight of the Gods	43
Belt It Round You	44
Through Silence	45
The One Who Guards Infinity	46
The Whelps of Judah	47
Such a Clever Monkey	48
The Heart of His Soul	49
Clouds like Cliffs	50
Time and You	51
Two Old Ravens	53
A Time of Thieves	55
Bring Us Up	57
There Comes…	58
The Winds of Time	59
Memorial Day	60
The Black Crepe	61
The Ruined Lord	62
Decorated	63
The Dream of Pride	64
Yet Forty Days and Nineveh Shall Be Overthrown	65
And Then He Stood Upright	66
We Dreamed That We Were Dead	67
The Prism	69
Emerging from the Sea	70
From the Start…	71
No More of Adam's Curse	72
As from My Emptiness	74
As I Climbed Up	75
Somewhere in Ukraine	77
Before Their Eyes	78
Some Looked Up	79
What May Come	80

Wisdom Is Her Name 81
What We Lost 82
Beside Your Steps. 83
As One of Them. 84
A Race of Angels 85
Some Great Fall 86
Go On 88
Make Them Tame. 89
Behold the Elevation 90
What Comes Next 91
At Morning Mass. 92
What Might Your Wishes Be? 93
The Sacred Word 95
The Rivers Ran Oil 96
So Bright 97
Did You Think?. 98
In Bethlehem 99
Are You Not Amazed? 100
Oh So Strange. 101
Until the Sky Is Ready 102
On the Mountains 103
Within the Fortress 104
None Can Guess. 105
Those Burning Bones 106

For Jonathan,
in courage and spirit

So Tell Us, Christ

Who believes the love of God
If one has been denied
The love of human beings first?
All love, stillborn has died

But then if God Himself is love
And He was crucified,
Christ foretells how love becomes
The breaching in His side

Love itself received the Cross
The hammer and the nail,
And if we crucify our love
Then love itself will fail

But if we offer love for love
It will rise up again,
So tell us Christ who rose for us
If love will rise, and when

The Break of Day

As birds sit on the wire
To watch the world below,
So the angels gathered
To see the cities glow

Isn't that the morning,
Servant of the Law?
Never such a morning,
A day you never saw

Go and tell the Master
The wonder of the change,
He already knows it
Although it is so strange

The glowing is a power
The city cannot hold,
All dominion weakness
And honesty is sold

Power has escaped them
To hover overhead,
Changed to desolation
The city of the dead

As birds who sit the wire
Leap and fly away
The angels lifted higher
To see the break of day

There was spread before them
The mountains and the sea,
Dawn that was a captive
Mounted and broke free

As He Loves the Jewel Starts to Blaze

Held by truth, their spirits turned to crystal,
This way, that way turned for God's appraisal,
He sees them through and through as if they were
A specimen of jewel to a jeweler

A property of preciousness He knows,
The quality, the luminance that glows
When He illuminates the facets of
A jewel of His worth, a gem of love

There is no room inside that stone for lies,
No way to hide, no matter what the size,
He is the jeweler, God artisan
Who made the soul to be with Him as one

He spins it round and round beneath His gaze
And as He loves, the jewel starts to blaze

Even in Old Babylon

Even in Old Babylon
On one day of the year,
The priest would slap the royal face
And pull the royal ears

The priest would then permit the king
To enter if so pleased
The sanctuary of the god
Although on hands and knees

So even at a pagan shrine
They knew humility
To be the ticket to behold
Such low divinity

Then how much more should we adore
The Christ of brilliant light
With self-effacing gentleness
Adoring and contrite

Where It Should

The petals of the pear tree blow
Across the garden of the blessed
Spinning lightly like the snow

All that lives in light is good
So when it falls it lightly falls
The tree has blossomed where it should

But that which serves opacity
Envious of all that lives
Consumes the heartwood secretly

The Curtain

The curtain of the inner sanctum
Hiding nothing clean, the Glory has departed
The veil is now an unclean kingdom

That sanctum is the holiness of Moloch
The ultrasonic piping of the bats
The mournful crowing of St. Peter's cock

When Christ undying rose up from the tomb
The useless veil was ripped in half
But a veil of light remains around Him

Who can bear to see the deathless One?
But in the Sacrifice of flesh and blood
He is the clouded and exalted sun

Where Love Has Gone

The light of faith a candle flame somewhere,
We hide it in a secret hiding place
Where love has gone, it is our own affair,
There is no map an enemy can trace

And yet there is no barrier or code
No secret password, document or plan,
No ruse or ambush likely to explode,
It is the candle of the Son of Man

Nothing puts it out except the will
Of One who lit it first, He is the Master,
Although a wind may blow the air is still
Where it is secreted from all disaster

It burns and ever burns and will burn yet
Though enemies may search the world for it

The Dust

God leaned across the Earth
As a man across a dusty table
And He blew the dust away

All envy, greed and pride
Flew up and out into
The dark abysses of the cosmos

Then the Earth was clean
Like a mirror that reflects
The superposed reflection of itself

The Lord recalled the dust
Assembled to an unlike pattern
From that which it had occupied

Let it try again, He said
Once more, another time
To draw itself up from itself

He named a different creature
That dust which struggled upright
To live another life

It is your name and mine
Of those who came before
Or those who will come after

He is the Lord of time and space
And He will name
Whomever He will name

Looking Down

Where I stand remain but few,
Come back with me to where I grew,
A ridge of tall and patient pines
And of these houses were no signs

But now I am alone with these,
A cawing crow, some other trees,
Beneath me are the graves of men
Of us not many specimens

But we will be their epitaph
And long the summer winds will laugh

Every Power

When we heard the fibers creak
We knew the tree had stopped the wind,
Ran without the breath to speak
For when it fell we might be pinned

Tulip poplar, tall and old
Fungus-rotted through and through,
Wind of winter rough and cold,
Desiccated, azure blue

If you hear the fibers crack
Then by reflex start and run,
Time has taken up its slack,
Suddenly your life is done

Unless you run—and this is true
That every power has its fall
When it has rotted through and through,
Though some may see no rot at all

When All the Wounds Cried Out

If every wound of ours would cry
The world would hear such great lament
That all the living would reply
To whom the Lord our Christ was sent

Down came He, took on the grief
Of love denied and love ignored,
On left and right a tortured thief
And from His side His mercy poured

Then He felt the pain and dread
Took on the grief that was unheard
By darkened minds and souls of lead—
He is the bright and living Word

Still the wounds cry out in pain
And He has means to offer cure,
The risen Christ will come again
But while we wait we must endure

Brief Spring

There are forces in creation,
Gravity and that which holds
The nucleus against repulsion,
Electroweak, which is two-fold

There is more we never see
More than that we may soon know,
A plan enfolds infinity
The world above, the world below

And you who see the flowering plum
The pear, the quince and all that flowers,
Remember that there is a sum
Of all the brief and passing hours

If and When

If and when we are relieved of sin,
Of greed and self-importance, loathsome skin,
Will it be painful to be stripped away
Against the tender spirit, will it flay?

Oh no, He said, I am more tender than
The softest woman and the gentlest man,
For when the skin of pride is taken off
It will by My devising be so soft

That like a glove removed without a pain
The skin will come away with every stain
To leave you uncorrupted and so pure
That you will be amazed, so is My cure

If your soul submits to Me with trust
I will remove from you that loathsome crust

Suddenly at Dawn and Since

Suddenly at dawn and since
Pear trees blossom and the quince
Around the mansions of the rich

Hedges of the berry briar
Grow around their branches higher
Rivers make a mound and ditch

The world has closed itself away
No matter what they do and say
No matter what they proffer, pay

Green will overgrow their walls
Until the rotting curtain falls
Dust of mortar rains around

Beneath the cupola of green
Dexterity and pride unseen
The vine and rootlet bring it down

Frost will wrench the bricks apart
Rain the sculptor works his art
Nothing of the house is left

Nothing of what money built
That will not suffocate in silt
Soft the stronghold built by theft

Then the woodland scraped and scoured
Limed and poisoned, burned and soured
Will by seed of seasons grow

When the geese of winter pass
Above the withered winter grass
Who that knew them then will know?

It Is Near

Scouts surveying the unknown
Saints and holy ones and prophets,
These explore the outer zone
Beyond the planets and the comets

Farther than the oldest stars
Galaxies and fields of dust,
Beyond where swarms of angels are,
The purgatory of the just

To where in loving perigee
The blessed souls in orbit stay,
Wherever light from light may be
The mystics travel, there are they

But for a moment, then they fall
From that alluring lost frontier
Which falsely the unknowing call
Impossible, though it is near

The Space of Nothing

His head was changed to a conical stub
A small eraser mixed with clay,
The body resembled you and me
But the noddle wiped the walls away

On it scratched a sort of face
But as it rubbed it disappeared
Until there was nothing left of him,
Death was not what he had feared

The wall removed him from the room
Or you might say he was sucked through
The space he made by rubbing out
The love of God that is proved true

For some there may be hell or not
Of that we living may not know,
But also winds of nothingness
That through the space of nothing blow

She Hates to See the Possums

She hates to see the possums
Gambol in Fox Hollow,
But foxes are the demon
Creatures of the shadows

One is a marsupial
Pocketed and fey,
The fox an elemental
More sinister than they

Heavy dusk at twilight
Dawn before the sun,
Most of all at midnight
The fox and vixen run

But once in a midwinter
In daylight through the snow
I saw a vixen canter
To startle mice below

Concealed from Whom?

Why does he take his firearm to church,
A gun that's light and small enough to pocket,
Concealed from whom, the angels?

He takes it everywhere, but why to God?
Crucified, the risen Lord invincible
Looks down and weighs his soul

For when they took Me to the Cross, He says
I did not bruise a reed, snuff out a wick
Isaiah tells the generations

Fearful ones, you make the world afraid—
Afraid of you, your enemies destroy you,
Shadows come around you and you shoot them

Beneath the Cross I see the weapons offered
High explosives, poison gas and fire
A thousand cities burning in the sanctuary

The blood of Christ drips down and steams like incense
The cries of burning children rise to Him—
Their parents cannot save them

This too is the present world's oblation
An offering as if the flesh of beasts
A bitter ceremonial

When I Awake Again

She happened in the cool bright night
The spirit of content,
Now rest, she said, as sleepers might
To whom my gift is sent

That all is well and as it goes
Have nothing to regret,
Lie sweetly in your long repose
Though waking you forget

And when the constellations fell
Beneath the western hill,
The rising sun approached, repelled
The darkness and the chill

But there was cold and cryptic fear
That I could not explain,
O Christ your Wisdom hover near
When I awake again

Tenebrae

Ierusalem, Ierusalem, convertere ad Dominum Deum tuum

Now the candles are extinguished
One by one, lament my city,
Truth and noble poverty
Love, self-giving charity

Peace and patience, homeliness
Modesty and cheerful grace,
Hope and faith and honesty
Mercy, justice interlaced

Benevolence and kindliness
Clemency and thankfulness,
Piety and decency
Each the joy that God will bless

See the blessings like the fingers
Folded in a human prayer,
Lights extinguished, Tenebrae
In the darkness Christ is there

In the darkness Christ is waiting
Offering a light to guide
Souls bewildered by the shadows
From the blindness of their pride

When I Showed...

When I showed the night my Easter candle
I offered up my soul, the little flame,
Insipid gift to God above the altar
Lost within the splendor of His name

Thinnest light beneath His utter star
Flame He can extinguish with a breath
Who gathers up the hurricanes of space
The greater wind of all that we name death

The cheapest candle sold, the cheapest wax
But something else the Risen bought tonight:
The ignorant receive the melted wax
But God has paid forever for the light

I Will Dip You in the Sky

If I were a redwood tree as tall as many spires
I would be intimate with clouds, the friend of many fliers,
My toes would grope beneath the ground, the coolness of it feel
The sun and moon go round my head, the stars a burning wheel

Although I might be slow of speech, the wind would serve as tongue
Thriftily my needles drink the air, enormous lung,
I would have lived with centuries and know them as my friends
My life would seem as long as hills' as though without an end

But even I, magnificent, my body thick and straight
A column in a temple green would still anticipate
The answer to a question, the puzzle of my soul
The slow and patient heart of me, O Lord what is my goal?

Could it be to root and grow the greatest of the tall?
Be of hope, my spirit says, though everything must fall,
You are as frail and breakable as any twig or straw
For I will dip you in the sky my images to draw

I Remember

Mystery do not retire
From the heartless and denier,
Unbelieving base betrayer
Hypocrite and spirit slayer

You have died for those as well
As saints confined within a cell,
Bore the whip for cheat and thief
Who devastate a child's belief

For cruel despots, savage masters
All who profit from disasters,
These you also died to save
Whose stronghold is a self-dug grave

Those inside the serpent's stone
The poisoned fruit of death, alone,
Even these you cause to live
For their contrition save, forgive

Forgive us in this Holy Week
Who know not well the love we seek,
For if we knew it we would know
The consolation You bestow

For I remember those who broke
An infant's back with savage strokes
And when the savers saw that child
He looked at those who came and smiled

The Men of Sodom

The men of Sodom ask for some ID
The enemies of human liberty,
Here is Sodom seeded from the past,
Rebuilt and renovated, made to last

The suitable perversion now is this:
A document subdermal in a cyst,
A constant electronic pheromone,
Transducer and a tracer and a phone

But still above the valley God surveys
The outrage of creation in those days,
The pleading of the patriarch in vain
To spare the wayward Cities of the Plain

Again a blinding light, the guests expose
Eternal light and bring them to a close

The Mighty Doors

Toward the Savior's Sacred Heart
Many crippled make their way
All who wish to be there may

Dawn within the chamber spreads
In His light the blind can see
Love's delight and majesty

Know how many gather there
Look around them, recognize
The beauty of the meek and wise

In the crossings of that Heart
Vaults and columns rise above
Assemblies of eternal love

Harmonious the blessed preach
Speechless ones can find their speech
Sing their blessing each to each

All are welcome to remain
But if there be a few who leave
Because for lack of love they grieve

And from His charity they flee
The mighty doors remain apart
In welcome to the Sacred Heart

Something Marvelous

If once you contemplate the dawn
And see the clouds configured there,
Amber, rose and wisps of wool,
The gray of dawn's nocturnal vair

Remember that when Jacob dreamed
Of angels' rising and descent,
The sky was just as this, the light
Fell shining from the firmament

And when the Nameless wrestled him
Scorpions had stirred their stings,
Desert birds inside their nests
Stretched and warmed their stiffened wings

All was as it is today
The color and the sense the same,
Except for something marvelous
That wrestled him but had no name

Or Was He Real?

Someone dead I never met but lately read about
Stood beside my easy chair in the coda of a dream
Solid as reality that lives and does not seem

Judging from the photographs his features disarranged
As if they had been glued together ill and hurriedly
In some infernal bucket shop or crazy factory

As if he were assembled from a load of unlike parts
According to a plan that's only partly understood
From realistic painted cloth and crooked scraps of wood

He held me in a skewed regard, his glasses at a tilt
And then as if a flickering that flashes on a wall
Vanished from my view as if he wasn't there at all

Something in that apparition makes me want to know
How much of our perception is assembled from the scraps
The little pieces manikins assemble in our naps

Put together in a sort of mock satiric way
By something old that gathers up the trimmings of our lapses
And sews them in confusion to the shreds of our synapses

Or was he real and do we see the recently departed
Paroled from their purgation uncompleted if we read
About them with some interest, then swiftly they recede

Pavel Chichikov

More Bright Than Many Suns

Melt snow, melt heart, melt flesh itself
We are the frozen ones,
Spirits of the Lord are swift
More bright than many suns

Then how can we become as they
If like a pinch of dust
Unburnable we blow away
Before a light can touch?

This is how it is devised:
God keeps us in His hand,
More sympathetic and more wise
Than we can understand

He says: You are My firefly
And when I let you go
You will be brilliant as am I
But with a lesser glow

The Elevation of the Host

The Elevation of the Host
The blessed light, infinity—
I wondered at the smallness of
The inner life and self of me

I dwindled to a point of time,
How insufficient as a host
Of life eternal, aught is mine,
I am a tendril, wisp, a ghost

He said: I will remove that husk
Which must disintegrate at last,
You creatures of the fleeting dusk
Between the future and the past

I will show the soul inside
As in this bread My corpus lives,
Sieve out your gross ungraceful pride
For that is what My grace forgives

The Falconry of Mammon

Those who keep a raptor for a pet
Sometimes suffer pitiful illusions
That falcons, hawks and eagles love them best
But these are birds of prey and love no one

Falcons fly when launched and then come back
Because they are conditioned to return,
But have no feelings or affections, lack
Emotions that a falconer might earn

So is there the falconry of mammon—
The loveless tie investments to the wrist
Which they may launch in flight to stoop upon
A victim profit fat with interest

But these are cold of eye, expressionless
And fastened loosely by a golden jess

Two Rivers

Water from under the altar
In a stream that no one sees,
The water becomes a river
The desert a grove of trees

A river waters the desert
But the desert only grows
The apples of desire
And yet the river flows

How can there be two rivers
Of death and fertility?
The one is the water of mercy
For the desert inside of me

Present Tense

A sign in a grassy field:
When nuclear war begins
The ban on school prayer will be lifted

The godless will call on God
Will pray penitential prayer
The criminals fall on their knees

That much will it take to bring
The hosts of millennium
To the gates of Jerusalem

And in the immediate fire
When flames have melted the streets
Truth will consume the denier

And they will have lived for once
In the light of the living God
The eternal present tense

The Groves of Glory

Seated at the banquet of the spirits
Some are not surprised by where they are
Who feast on truth and happiness forever
Who feast with deep and pleasurable hunger
Appeased though ever whetted by their joy

But some who were the dull and bitter ones
Will be surprised at where and how they are
Look around them as they gaze at music
Listen to the colors of the banquet
Taste its welcome as it were a nectar

For they had been restrained and put in prison
By one who must despise his limitation
That powerful in evil he may be
He cannot make a single joy or welcome
Create a life or else take pleasure in it

But those who come to heaven will awaken
As if from some profound and healing sleep
And they will gaze in joy at those around them
Refreshed beside the waters of the Boundless
Beneath the groves of glory and of peace

The Strangest Thing of All

I tell you of the strangest thing of all
How love can come to love beyond a wall
For love can love the infant held in arms
And love can love the child who comes to harm
Love can love the father and the mother
Siblings and the helpless and all others
Love can love the lover for her grace
Or love her for the sweetness of her face
Love can love the absent who return
Love is given, taken but not earned

But this is stranger far than love for those
Love can love the one who dies and goes
Goes beyond the visible and high
For we can love the ones we love who die
And if we thought them vanished into dust
We would not want to love them, but we must

He May Reply

An angel took me up and showed
The fire that the angel sowed,
Seeds of fire in a field,
Seeds of wrath that he unsealed

I asked: When will these seedlings bear
The flames of some deserved despair?
He said: As Sodom will become
The burning of your kingdoms come

He said: When Samson set ablaze
Tails of foxes in those days
Of ancient Israel that was such
A fire that the world will touch

Then the fields of growing grain
Now the cities of the plain,
Around the circle of the sphere
The blazing of the atmosphere

I asked: Is there a way to stop
The growing of this burning crop?
He said: I am a creature sent
To compensate the innocent

Above all else for this repaid:
The children burned in fire raids;
"Save me mother for I burn"
For this God's vengeance you will earn

I asked: Is there a way to halt
This punishment against our fault?
The angel paused and then replied:
Ask One who for these children died

There is less time than you can know
For even now these seedlings grow,
Appeal to Him, He may reply
But who knows how He will, not I

All Admired Babylon

All admired Babylon, but Babylon recedes
Babylon the mighty is overwhelmed by weeds,
Towers crack and crumble like maggot-sickened bread
The city that was strident is the city of the dead

But still an army swaggers up and down the street
Merchants come together to falsify and cheat,
They haggle and they swindle though long ago deceased
Servants set a table at the graveside for a feast

I was once in Babylon many years ago
Saw the mighty ziggurat illuminated glow,
Cast around the city a dome of lurid light
But light projects the shadows to intensify the night

From these deepest shadows a pestilence came out
Greed and great indifference, depravity and doubt

Where They Wait

The people of the sky appeared last night
Their bodies mottled azure blue
The white of scattered clouds
But since their bodies blend against the sky
They are invisible to all except the few

No one will commend them, they have few friends
Since hardly anyone can tell
Where they begin and brightness ends
They are slowly dying as a race
As storms appear, of them there is no trace

But they will manifest to those who wait
Sometimes years and decades till they come
To show themselves in solitary places
The edges of a lucid dream perhaps
But even then one may not see their faces

Here is what I know of them, they are not fire
But they have knowledge of where fire glows
They ride the wind that canters from the west
And to the east when day has weakened go
But where they wait for light again nobody knows

And yet I think they pity us and now foresee
From loftiness what others may not see
A heightened risk of some calamity
Which we in lower space do not suspect
Because we know not where we go nor can detect
The cross of roads where corollaries intersect

Where Is He?

He told us: Wait, I come again
Transformed Himself through bread and wine
And then appeared to Paul, and then

His life in us a present grace
Appeared in love that gives itself,
Love's affections interlaced

So that the monks in capitals
Drew thickets where His creatures hide
Herbs adorning animals

Comes again and still once more
Until like summer's heavy rain
Love and graces pour

Where has He gone and why so late
This promised sacrament returned?
But it is Christ Himself who waits

Pavel Chichikov

The Twilight of the Gods

Little moth, the opera is in progress
See, the doors are open, flutter in,
Down an aisle above the many seats
Do you see the colors, hear the music?

No, there is a cavern and a sunless warmth
Currents rising, falling and a breath of wind
Vibration in the air and amplitudes
To make the membranes of my wings pulsate

Don't you understand the clever story?
Love and vengeance, treachery, a golden ring,
Power for a sacrifice of human love
Renunciation till the end of time

No, there's nothing in it but some roominess
Sunless beaming of a light, exotic smells

Listen then, my little one, those others here
Know no more of God than you of this

Belt It Round You

What are we being readied for?
The mood is militant, defensive
The prospect is of war

As ever when the die is cast
The tempo rises of belligerence
Until the heart beats fast

I thought I saw my uncle then
Returning from another war
Which had devoured many men

And I a small child meeting him
The corner of our peaceful street
And he not even hurt or grim

And in his pack were souvenirs
Machine gun bullets and a Luger—
He'd left behind him all his fear

Discarded ownerless somewhere
Until another found it, put it on—
Belt it round you if you dare

Through Silence

There is a time, a time of God
When every creature stops and waits,
Time itself has halted, then
Each sentience that God creates

Listens and detects the stroke
Of every pulse and every thought,
The inhalation of the light
Which animates what God has sought

All become aware of all
Each anima aware of each,
So down comes every block and wall
That through the silence all may reach

The One Who Guards Infinity

The one who guards infinity said this:
As many grains of light as he will need
To grow the grain of being that exists
Are given to the gardener as seed

To plant the light in loam of memory
And when it grows existence is the crop,
The harvest gathered in is harmony
And never will the gathering be stopped

This is how the world is made to be
And I am here to guard it and profess
The crop of light, the everlasting tree
For I am one of His and tireless

To see that every grain of love is kept
Immaculate, the harvest never done,
But everything that fails to love is swept
Into a bottomless oblivion

The Whelps of Judah

I saw the lions mass and run
Across an unknown plain, their flanks
Were pressed against each other and
They moved as one in rows and ranks

What lions are these, sir, I said
And when can I stand farther back
To see the rising of the dead,
The glory which the world has lacked?

On no, he said, this is no end
But first there must be massacre
When no one can the wealth defend
Within the whitewashed sepulcher

Their capital was bones and skin
Prosperity putrescent meat,
The whelps of Judah have grown thin
And now they starve and wish to eat

Such a Clever Monkey

There used to be a saying
A Chinese apothegm,
A monkey in the road
Can stop ten thousand men

See the column halted
The army is spellbound,
Such a clever monkey
We put our weapons down

We have seen the monkey
Who stops an army dead,
Here we will be halted
In regiments of lead

The Devil is the monkey
Who capers in disguise,
Such a clever monkey
To keep us paralyzed

The Heart of His Soul

A tumor is growing inside you, I said—
What kind of tumor and where does it lie?
Death is the tumor, division from God
Deeper and blacker the more you deny

Deeper and blacker and less of you lives
Although in your mirror you seem to be vast
Until you have dwindled to dust in the light
Then darker and smaller die into the past

The sign of diminishment often is this:
Bile in the eye and venomous tongue,
Blindness to beauty but hunger for praise
Contempt for the simple and fondness for dung

Who is the surgeon who cuts out this mass,
When does he operate, can he start soon?
He is the surgeon who offers Himself
The heart of His soul, the blood of His wounds

Clouds like Cliffs

Clouds like cliffs above the hills
Fog through which a gray light pours
A call of geese above the mist

If we could see above these clouds
An echelon of shouting birds
Would seem to row across the sky

If you and I could see right through
The clouds that cover up the world
It would reveal an exodus

Every spirit hatched from death
Rising up to join the blessed
That fly because they can forgive

Time and You

Summer night and windless, warm
When I went walking in the sea
I thought my God had forgotten me

From Corsica came choppy waves
Low and ivory-fretted foam
Across the shoreline coming home

Down the shore the River Jucar
Spread its crest along the sea
Nothing in the waves knew me

Either then go forward, back
Through darkness of a light untrue
Because the muffled moon was new

But someone said not for a while
Because I am not finished yet
Go landward let the dark moon set

It, not me, unfinished yet
With what the voice had made of me
Who walked by darkness through the sea

For if one wades out far enough
The buoyancy lifts up the mass
And then the weightless through it pass

To leave that earthly weight is such
A strong desire of the fugue
Of loss that turns to lassitude

Those who know the viscid wish
To cast away the robe of dread
Will know why they turn back instead

Two Old Ravens

Two old ravens in a tree
Looked down on a battlefield,
The older said: See what I see?
I think a truth has been revealed

Remember when they had no souls?
No, the other said, but you
Can tell what ancient mountains told
When they looked down and Earth was new

I tell you they were peaceable
Except when there was scarcity
Of food or females, all was well,
The violence flared up fleetingly

Once the beasts had souls they kept
Their malice burning day and night
Like fire in a smothered pit,
Their cunning kept it out of sight

But when it flared it burned and burned
Until it burned their places down,
It even makes my stomach turn
And I take pickings where they're found

Was it the soul inside that bled,
The wound that made them so insane?
It may be so, the older said,
When they could give their lust a name

When they changed from soulless beast
Into a soulful animal
Their purity as creatures ceased
And there was born the criminal

The ravens stood and rubbed their beaks
Across the limb where they had sat,
Then they spread their wings to seek
The beasts who burn their cities flat

A Time of Thieves

They swung their heavy hammers
Smashed the plate glass windows
Took a hundred Rolexes

The wheelman picked them up
Then they rode somewhere
Perhaps to Baltimore or anywhere

But no one can steal time
Only diamond watches
Time may not be stolen

Time inviolate
Time the everlasting
Until it ends

So that the robbers' fence
Will pay them ten per cent
And the money will run out

Money buys no time
But time will spend them well
It is no miser

Let us purchase time
Say all the money thieves
But time is not for sale

If someone robbed some time
Wound it in a watch
The watch would seize and stop

They would cease to run
But time would travel on
And leave them there

Bring Us Up

The trees are waking from their sleep
Whose roots have tunneled fathoms deep
And touched the larva, mole and grub
With bristle, knuckle, bend and nub

And so confirmed to be alive
The living that will rise and thrive,
While they comb out their tender hair
With fingers of the southern air

On the limb a wordless note
That some believe an empty rote,
But these are lessons taught by love
From deepest root to branch above

Which is the best of any prayer
To sing the light in wordless air,
Say: Be of us and we will bathe
In all Your beauty and be brave

There Comes...

There comes the wretched prodigal, the ne'er-do-well
The one that everybody said had gone to hell,
Rags for clothes, no shoes at all and one black eye
I guess wherever he got to the well ran dry

There's the Dad with cleaner clothes, a fancy ring
Gold I think and solar systems glittering,
Sentimental fool, a hug and tears run down,
He'd better stop that blubber or the kid will drown

That's a good one, look at how they pour the wine
The way the dancers pound their feet is not refined,
Don't you hate their gushiness, it makes me cringe
And every time I do it makes the fire singe

The Winds of Time

The angle of the study heads southwest
So that in March the window lets the light
Come streaming from the morning in a column
That leaves the window fading to the right

Later on, three quarters after three
Sunlight floods in glory as before,
Golden on the window plants and pours
Golden bars against the wooden floor

The study is a ship that ploughs ahead
Through time as if a vessel on a reach
Of golden light to find a port of call
Above a golden harbor and a beach

There the souls are walking to and fro,
The winds of time refreshing as they blow

Memorial Day

The hillside filled with flags that wave like grass
Gravesides swept and garnished with remembrance,
Monday is the day of reminiscence,
Wind has clasped the graves in its embrace

Who preserves the resonances, keeps
Precisely in their minds the wars that fade?
When they lived the flags above the streets
Quickened with their colors their parades

Visitors bring symbols to this hill—
The graves of those so lovingly they tend
With flags are void, no spirit may be killed,
The wars are buried here and not the men

The Black Crepe

We may yet see the world in funeral crepe
Streamers of blackness from burning cities
So that from above the blue is blocked
The night side spreading to both her sides

And the moon looks down, wrote Robinson Jeffers,
She says: My sister, what ails you so?
A wretched scurf from the mites on my skin
An inflammation that soon will clear

Then you will face my seas again
Cold and healthy with curds of foam
The shallows bright with flowering coral
But first the crepe of the black cremation

Must this be? Said the moon to her sister
Her silver cheeks against the sun,
I am prepared my sister dear
And have been since they scored my skin

The Ruined Lord

If you were ever broken, the pieces are still there,
Try and pick them up again if you should ever care,
Put yourself together from fragments on the ground,
Stand erect on sutured legs, be sure to look around

See the others mended although they always hide
Fractures of the inner self, the damages inside,
Was ever such an army as invalids like these
Battered and forsaken rising from their knees?

As Jesus healed the lepers and vivified the dead
Wine made up from water, the famished many fed,
So He puts together what agony has broken,
Jesus is the ruined Lord come back again as token

Decorated

He wrote to all the blogs and on-line papers
Demanding war against some other country
And every time he did another skull
Was hung around his neck by grinning demons

A skull with skin attached and shreds of flesh
Bonus for his bloody dedication,
Invisible except to fiends of hell
And weightless in this world, though not another

More and more and heavier and heavier
Each son, each father lost became a head
To hang around the neck of that warmonger
The decorated eater of the dead

The Dream of Pride

He said: The door is open,
I thought I saw it there,
A portal into heaven
Opened in the air

A doorway or a window,
Beyond it I could see
Four rivers and a garden,
A splendid fruiting tree

The sunlight on the rivers
Was like an aureole
That sanctifies and covers
The blessing of the soul

Jacob dreams a ladder
Between the earth and sky,
But he can climb it never
Heaven is too high

Paradise descended
Where angels rose and fell,
Heaven condescended
His destiny to tell

But now the portal closes
And seldom opens wide
As Paradise disposes
Against the dream of pride

Yet Forty Days and Nineveh Shall Be Overthrown

They listened and believed him,
The marvel of it all,
For many hear but do not heed
A prophesied downfall

Others do not even hear
The noises in the street,
They flourish in a deafness till
A downfall is complete

Anyone is justified
To say this is a tale
About the inescapable,
Folk wisdom and a whale

Others might identify
A sort of bleak acumen,
Oftener than oftener
The city comes to ruin

Nineveh attended once
But ultimately fell,
We are the inheritors
Succumbing to a spell

Jonah has posterity
Prefiguring no lie,
But all the fattened citizens
Deny, deny, deny

And Then He Stood Upright

By the end of a bitter winter
The frost goes down a meter,
Admit the soul is ground
How far can frost go down?

Can the life be lost,
Repel a killing frost?
Take love away, such chill
Can grip the soul and kill

If deeper, deeper goes
The clutching of the snows
The life of us will stop
And never make a crop

Never hope to raise
The flower of God's praise;
Then what can bring a thaw?
The One who Mary saw

The garden green at dawn,
Across the earth was drawn
A rod of living light
And then He stood upright

We Dreamed That We Were Dead

The world rose up from sleep
When Christ rose from the tomb
But now it sleeps again

Those who would not wake
In the garden of Gethsemane
Turn away in dreams

Who keeps vigil now?
Christ alone prepares,
Watches in the garden

The gibbous moon shines out
And gives a brilliant light
And the stars withdraw

Although the moon is bright
Shining in their faces
They turn away and sleep

It is the human race
That must arise from death
When death is conquered

When He comes again
Everyone will wake
Remembering their dreams

We dreamed that we were dead
But Christ rose from the grave
And we awoke

The Prism

Simple is the white of snow
Containing every color
But if I look for elements
Simplicity won't measure

A prism held against the light
Will separate the tones
From violet to green to red
That seemed as white alone

Are the colors made of white
Or white of all the hues?
I unify or separate
Exactly as I choose

If I search for signs of God
I split or unify,
So I may confirm His grace
Or if I wish deny

He is in the unity
And also in the schism,
Harmony the life of God
And wonder is the prism

Emerging from the Sea

If thinking is an instinct
Like walking up a hill,
Like swallowing and drinking
Like eating up your fill

The blinking of an eyelid,
Drawing at a straw,
Would the mind be mindful
According to a law?

Thinking is the plover
Not knowing where it goes,
Born to be a rover
The way a river flows

Thought is like the pigeon
From Noh's menagerie
That landed on a mountain
Emerging from the sea

From the Start...

From the start of everything
On this you can depend,
Starting is not finishing
The end is not the end

Nothing ends despite the throes
Of one side or the other,
There's a thing the devil knows
Never utter never

Those who watch the world on high
Seldom interfere
Even when the simple die,
Calamity draws near

Let a soldier shoot a gun
There will be a battle,
God is no automaton
The angels are not cattle

Peace has never been the spread
When war is on the plate,
Judas took a piece of bread
And flesh is what he ate

No More of Adam's Curse

Tell me truly what will they resemble
The souls in paradise when they assemble?
Beautiful as birds of paradise
Those fortunate to have been given twice
To God's good mercy and the light of grace?
What will their natures be in that bright place?

Nothing that the visionless can be
In shadowland where seeing doesn't see;
No one knows among the race that fell
What citizens of paradise could tell
If those who live on Earth would comprehend
What lies beyond the Alpha and the end

But this I think I know and you might too,
Imagine what the folk of Eden knew,
That all is one, most beautiful, eternal
Never old but always fresh and vernal,
No barrier there was between the dream
And consciousness, they did not have that seam

That all is one and they were one with all
As ever bright as spring with no nightfall,
That what they saw and praised is what they spoke
Before the oneness of creation broke;
Such will paradise resemble still
When unity of love will be fulfilled

But more than this, the barrier between
What spirits say and what they feel and mean
Will be dismantled and the souls converse
In harmony, no more of Adam's curse
That he within and everyone outside
Would never touch, his fullest love denied

As from My Emptiness

Improbable to see five thousand men
Sitting on a lawn, not more among
Them than two loaves, two perch split-dried
Hanging from the cord on which they're strung

So then the wonder rabbi feeds them all
As if the air had wallets or the clouds
Dropped the food from somewhere out of mind—
You'd either scratch your head or laugh out loud

I dreamed it did I? Yet I saw it done
As from my emptiness these words are drawn
As if five thousand hungry men were told
To have some faith and sit down on the lawn

As I Climbed Up

As I ascended Golgotha
At first the hill seemed low
And easy to go up but then
Somehow ascent was slow

So that what should have taken less
Than minutes was prolonged,
Steeper was the grade of it,
My legs and wind less strong

And as the morning sun drew up
The heat increased in power,
A climb I thought would soon be done
Became a climb of hours

The hill became a pinnacle
Forsaken, full of stones
That cut the feet and ankles
And knocked against the bones

The farther that I scrambled up
The higher grew the peak
Where at the top I saw someone,
The One for whom we seek

O Christ this climb is hard on me
And higher grows the hill,
Will I be never done with this
Exhaustion of the will?

The longer and the higher up
No closer seems the Cross,
But you are here, I heard Him say
Your climbing is no loss

It seemed as far to Me, He said
As hard and hot and dry,
And you will reach your cross at last,
And it will be as high

Somewhere in Ukraine

Somewhere in Ukraine, some year
Yet unborn you won't remember
In your far unknowing future

But I see for you, in the street
Blood poured out from skull to feet
A crumpled man like surplus meat

Although at end of every war
We said that we will have no more
And so in penitence we swore

But we are born recidivists
Homicides and hypocrites
Animals with brains and fists

And so I send this visual
Of murder not unusual
Your ancestors were criminal

And pray that you have been released
From slaughter and have got your peace
Or else posterity has ceased

Before Their Eyes

He said: my mother has been stricken,
Years ago began to sicken,
Dementia overtakes her mind,
What torment has your God designed?

There is no God and no I Am,
He said, but still I say goddamn,
If I should meet Him I will tell
That tormenter to go to Hell

I remembered how I once
Had suffered grief for someone else
And questioned why if kingdom come
There is such empty martyrdom

I kneeled before the Holy Child
Of Prague and all was reconciled,
For there was much that is, will be
The blessed spirits know and see

But how can ever one convey
The mystery I saw that day?
Who knows? The scroll of light is sealed
And to the very small revealed

But as for those consumed by rage,
Not till the ending of the age
When all the dead must live and rise
Will it unroll before their eyes

Pavel Chichikov

Some Looked Up

Some who climbed the rough-hewn plank
Looked up to see the curving ark,
Others in their nervous ranks
Waited while the sky turned dark

Which of us is waiting now
For rescue as the sky grows dim,
The sun falls down in spreading glow
Against the Earth's enormous limb?

Some have thought this just a tale
An ethno-mythic parable,
A legend or a tribal veil
Drawn across a chronicle

Always there are refugees
Fleeing from a field of war
And natural calamities
As there have always been before

But now I think of greater gauge
And powers we have summoned up,
Stupendous violence we have waged
The vicious pride of the corrupt

There need not be another rain
Or punishment that God exacts,
Behold the clouds of wrath again
And who can say the warrant lacks?

What May Come

A man whose hobby is to build
Bird houses though there are no birds,
So those who write although not skilled
Nail and hammer at their words

Who thinks the birds will someday perch
By spring at least or maybe summer,
The dowel oak, the sides are birch
The roof what he can glue together

What will come he can't foretell,
He hopes to hear the tenants sing,
But what may come no one can tell
For who knows what the sky will bring?

Wisdom Is Her Name

In all her complex weavings
In the forethought of her stratagems
In the subtleties of patience
Shaped by all necessities
In exquisite, elaborate detail
Coded step by step in her determined plan
Is it so?

The code is somewhere elsewhere logical
Enfolding and all-purposeful
In her, in us, in everything and everywhere

What is she then?
Do you see the web
The interlocking spiral threads?

One like her, the spider, catches wings
Although it too is subject to the algorithm
And to it linked as silken cable is
But she, the Spirit's artifice, detains the soul
Wisdom is her name

What We Lost

Who told them they were blessed
When the Lord God gave them Paradise?
They were simple, effortless

All the creatures never fallen
Lived as one beneath the shade of trees
The undivided ecstasy of heaven

The sword and fire of forgetfulness
Banished them from holy unison
They could not see beyond their own distress

And here the creatures also die
Devour one another as we do
And the trees are sick with longing for the sky

Beside Your Steps

The hills have spoken and the trails
Unwind the tracks of fox and doe
Which weigh near nothing on the scale
That weighs the heavy weight of snow

We are so strong we prop the sky,
So old that ages fall like rain
And run away though they may try
To wear us down to seas again

When you came here and printed text
With freezing, melting, sinking script
We shrugged, the feet that came here next
Into the morgue of ages slipped

Can you mean no more than this,
The tracks the beasts print on our backs?
You are much more mysterious,
Beside your steps another track

As One of Them

Whom He loves our Savior breaks
As He broke on the cross,
What sense in what He suffered then?
Whose pain was it, whose loss?

Did Jesus not forsake Himself
When giving sacrifice?
What price for this abandonment
Which suffered paid no price?

But children have no debt to pay
Why do they suffer so?
Grief and torment is the way
That some must undergo

But when they ask why is this pain,
The blameless have no pride,
Say reason falters once again
As one of them He died

A Race of Angels

Above, in these primeval hills
New water runs through fossil seas,
Evaporates, deposits crusts
Of calcium the water frees

How many clumsy beasts kicked through
Those old uplifted bottomlands
Beneath an ocean, ever changed
Before transmuting to a man?

From tusk to tail until at last
Upright and clever, stubborn-wise
A race emerging from the past
How many aberrations died?

God is patient yet contrived
Another race angelic, fleet
As thought, as vital and alive
A human beings, though complete

He made them perfect from the start
No evolution was required
And yet much closer to his heart
The flawed mutations He desired

For as the angels brilliant be,
To fire as is flesh to frost,
So even dull and sluggish we,
Not one He loves is ever lost

Some Great Fall

The dam is fifty meters tall
Of solid granite obdurate,
So from the walkway in his fall

He thumped the angles of the stones
Hit the bottom where he lay
With no apparent broken bones

But he was dead and this is how:
Each organ in the body fixed
By membranes from the cleft to brow

Was ripped away and so he died,
Although he seemed unhurt without
The organs were detached inside

You could have rattled him and heard
A sound of organs jumbled up
Like pebbles shaken in a gourd

Society may seem intact
But if the soul is disengaged
So that no part can interact

Unless it jostles other parts—
The separate mind uncoupled is
From grace and spirit, soul and heart

It was the impact violent
Of some great fall that made it so
And none have since been innocent

Go On

The sun went down, and all the ways grew dark
        —The Odyssey, trans. D. C. H. Rieu

The ways grow dark this winter dusk
And soon alone, each one astray
Go where you will, you will be lost,
None who came will know the way

The signs were switched, the maps are false
The mission given was a lie
That sends you to your death or else
The ones you left behind will die

We heard a thunder growing near
Or we ourselves approached the sound,
No one knows what could appear
Behind the darkness all around

The orders say with confidence
Our plans are working and by dawn
There will be victory, immense
Successes will be ours, go on

Make Them Tame

The tracks of rabbits in the snow
That cut across, diagonals,
Seldom do we see them though

Cottontails avoid our sight
There before and afterward
Though it be day, though it be night

They say the weak outlast the strong
But meanwhile long of life are those
Who hold the power—Lord how long?

But this is how, the weak evade
The potency that must erode,
Their might, their strength is overplayed

That leads the great to self-defeat
Exhaustion, even boredom wins,
Their triumph never made complete

But like the rabbits, so the meek
Who live unnoticed as does Christ,
The innocent whom Herod seeks

That being so, the strong proclaim:
We will domesticate the weak
And make them tame

Behold the Elevation

Behold the Elevation of the Host
A prologue and a little preparation
To bring the festal dinner of the blessed

Lovers at the banquet who will feast
Upon the open glory of the mighty One
A celebration that will never cease

But one who sat at table rose and said
What about the little ones on Earth
Abused and broken, love-starved and so seldom fed

The voice was not a low and cringing treble
But rose above the singing of the psalms
Nor was the questioner a probing devil

And then for many moments there was kept
Great silence as the Glory showed His face
That was the battered Crucified, He wept

And then the vision faded and I thought
My Christ I cannot bear it yet You did
Such agony of pity that You sought

What Comes Next

The snow said print your footsteps here
Then came the quail, the fox, the deer

With hoof and pad and toe and claw
That all was published by the law

Afterward a war to write
With shell, grenade and laser sight

Rocket salvos tracked their feet
On fields that once had grown gold wheat

I saw those letters black as soot
Where guns had stamped a burning foot

But then survivors, scavengers
Would scatter these until they blurred

Peruse in haste this blotted text
Before the spring and what comes next

At Morning Mass

At morning Mass were just a few
But for a moment many more
Were sitting there behind my pew

At ease and watching with content
The Eucharistic sacrament
The transformation imminent

Behind me for I sat ahead
The vanished ones for whom I prayed
The confident immortal dead

Yes we are the ones who died
Waiting for the golden One
We would by this be satisfied

They were there, I could not see
Their faces for I did not turn
But they had come to sit with me

But in a moment they were gone
And I began to beat my breast
To finish our eleison

What Might Your Wishes Be?

He came up over the Moore's Hill ridge
Just as the winter sun was rising
Red shadows on a thin snow cover

It takes some guts to hike alone
Even if your wind is good
A titanium valve is in his heart

Bitter cold in January
Along the foothills and the scarps
Of the rolling Alleghenies

When the trail has narrowed in
There's not much room to place a foot
On the rough and glassy ridge

Once at the foot of another ridge
Climbing up in waist-deep snow
It was so cold to stop was death

At dusk's blue end I saw two mink
Tumbling, romping in the drifts
As the night cold squeezing tested me

Face to face to meet blue death
And then pass by and say farewell
Means you have to go alone

Sometimes there's an urge to see
And meet whatever stands and waits
To ask: What might your wishes be?

The Sacred Word

Before the second coming
The dawn before that day
There sat an angel on a stone
A pearwood lute to play

What is the music, angel
And what might you be called?
I am the angel Gabriel
Today the world must fall

This is a suite of Johann Bach
I play before the end
I love the taking of the strings
The melodies they send

They are like the world of light
In which all melodies
Resound together on the lute
I made from pearwood trees

Then he struck the final chord
And sang the sacred text
The sky became a sacred word
The angel uttered next

The Rivers Ran Oil

The Tigris, Euphrates
A male and a female
Flowing from Eden
Before the great Fall

Joined at the ocean
Scented with attar
Of olive and date
Of fig, oleander

Spread to the seas
A copious scent
To make the earth teem
Those bountiful currents

Beasts became numerous
Forests spread wide
Through the lands of the Earth
Before there was pride

But when the first couple
Chose willful dishonor
Instead of delight
There was fire and terror

Ousted from Eden
To an exile of toil
They dug in the ground
And the rivers ran oil

So Bright

To the top I go
To meet the Northern Clipper
To wait for Lady Snow
Her soft and silent slipper

But that must be tonight
The sky is laced with blue
Gray and brilliant white
The wind has blown askew

Not even crows have flown
Since morning or have called
But light itself has grown
So bright that it can scald

Did You Think?

Ice rain, cold rain, winter rain
Steady rain, white rain, clear rain
Black rain, sleet rain

It will freeze and will not thaw
No salt will melt it, liquefy
That slick hard surface

This is not rain at all
But the armor of the human heart
Cold and impervious

Or did you think that rain is only rain?

In Bethlehem

Have you heard that God is born today?
But He is God and will not bear that way

Have you seen Him mewling in the straw?
Infants weep, do not inspire awe

Was there not above the crib a star?
A stall below and God is always far

Is He not the Son of the eternal?
The cosmos is the shell and God the kernel

Do not majesties approach to praise?
The Christ must come but possibly delays

Is He not foretold in prophecy?
He will be fierce and bring an armory

Let me show you what will be His tomb
Beneath the walls of Zion there is room

For all that is and ever there will be,
In Bethlehem immortal infancy

Are You Not Amazed?

Do you know me, I am your
Son who made you, I am born
The offspring of a carpenter
Given over to the scorn

Of many but the ragged few
Whom I selected as my friends,
Caiaphas knew not of you
The priestly money that they spent

To bribe a traitor to betray
Would better have been spent on bread
To feed the multitude but they
Knew me not till I was dead

But here I am, the foster son,
The infant Jesus that you raised
Who now becomes the Risen One—
Joseph are you not amazed?

Oh So Strange

He likes to fish, said Peter's wife
He won't catch much but who can tell
And who can stop him, off he goes
With that crew of ne'er-do-wells

His heart is broken and he's scared
But fishing calms him well enough,
The sea is quiet until dawn,
By afternoon it can be rough

There he goes to ease his heart
The water peaceful, there it lies
By quarter moon before the dawn,
A current takes the boat coastwise

Fist and haul the empty net
To mend the meshes where it frayed,
Shoreward slowly they ride in
Though counting fish they might have stayed

Nothing ever really changes
Dreams that happened floating free,
It won't come back but oh so strange
The figure on the beach they see

Until the Sky Is Ready

The power at work so quietly
That we never hear the sunrise
Or the footfall sound at dusk

We are the incomplete
Unfinished sentence
Bated breath

I saw great dusk display
Fluorescent fire opal
Burning primrose in the west

The lights are on in the valley
The winter hills unfinished
Until the sky is ready

On the Mountains

As the dew falls lightly
The Spirit of God on the hills
The sweet valleys

So on my soul
Fertile or sterile, never at peace
Except in your presence

So in that place
The Lord's appearance
Grace upon grace

What will there be
When the dew has fallen
Above and below?

In the valleys peace
The grain of God
On the mountains, snow

Within the Fortress

A clear fine day in middle spring,
On rising ridges five miles off
Single trees reveal themselves

But as the locust sconces blossom
White and lilac pendant clusters
And as the clover blooms its wool

There are no bees to forage here
A desolation, holocaust—
Is there no one to see and fear?

They are the sentinels of God
Withdrawing from their outer posts
As we within the fortress feast

None Can Guess

As if now summoned she alights again
Broad of shoulder, tapering of wing
And how should we who see her know her name?

The creatures on the ground are not afraid
One small beast approaches her and sniffs
Stretches out as if it had been tamed

I see her on the fence from where I sit
A soul of wing and steel from those deep draughts
That flow in icy currents on her breast

As I have summoned one who seemed like her
In mental picturing, this day she comes
As powerful as then in fledging dress

But when full-fledged what messenger is she
And on what day will she alight, arrive?
That time will be which none of us can guess

Those Burning Bones

I saw St. Peter's church on fire,
The stolid congregation stayed,
Flame from pew to wall to choir,
How could they be not afraid?

There they sat by rank and file
Smoke around them rising thick,
Shouting I ran down the aisle,
Along the walls the fire licked

Pull the people from their places
Bodies motionless as stones
With rigid and unfeeling faces:
"Burnt you will be only bones."

Get out and save yourself, I heard
They will not move till Kingdom come
And Christ returns as was His word
For these are stupid, deaf and dumb

But then as in Ezekiel
I heard another in command
Above the desecration tell
Those burning bones to live and stand

Pavel Chichikov is the pen name of a writer who lives in a small town in central Pennsylvania. He has written for Catholic media and also for the secular press on such issues as Soviet nuclear weapons systems and Soviet environmental problems. His books include *Lion Sun: Poems by Pavel Chichikov* (Grey Owl Press, 1999), *Mysteries and Stations in the Manner of Ignatius* (Kaufmann Publishing, 2005), *From Here to Babylon* (Grey Owl Press, 2010), and *A House Rejoicing* (Grey Owl Press, 2012).

His work from 1993 to date is archived electronically and in print at the library of Ave Maria University, Ave Maria, Florida, along with newspaper clippings, published books, recorded readings, and personal papers.

His poetry is presented every week on his Website: www.pavelspoetry.com. His poems about the Spanish painter Francisco Goya can be seen at www.homagetogoya.com, and his photography is presented at pavel.romancatholic.org.

www.ingramcontent.com/pod-product-compliance
Lightning Source LLC
Chambersburg PA
CBHW051656040426
42446CB00009B/1170